CUTTING ROOM

SARAH PINDER

COACH HOUSE BOOKS, TORONTO

first edition

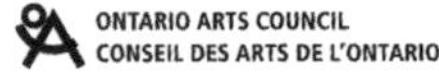

Canadä

Published with the generous assistance of the Canada Council for the Arts and the Ontario Arts Council. Coach House Books also acknowledges the support of the Government of Canada through the Canada Book Fund and the Government of Ontario through the Ontario Book Publishing Tax Credit.

LIBRARY AND ARCHIVES CANADA CATALOGUING IN PUBLICATION

Pinder, Sarah, 1983-
Cutting room / Sarah Pinder.

Poems.
Issued also in an electronic format.
ISBN 978-1-55245-264-6

I. Title.

PS8631.I51C88 2012 C811'.6 C2012-904678-7

Cutting Room is available as an ebook: ISBN 978 1 77056 324 7.

Purchase of the print version of this book entitles you to a free digital copy. To claim your ebook of this title, please email sales@chbooks.com with proof of purchase or visit chbooks.com/digital. (Coach House Books reserves the right to terminate the free digital download offer at any time.)

fuel

one street named after a saint or mountain, another after blood,
pealing bells, loose live gerunds strung across, pitched in hum,
every eye a question, a pan, an establishing shot.

the alternate ending: wreck this, move with speed, a leash,
obedient click and what follows, wagging, eager, full breath

after the foot lifts, the cloud of upper sound in flat wet midday
warmth. you want drag in chorus, field spent, the clench of taking
aim at exhausted scrap, blowing it all –
the name of a pocket, a hand-carved tattoo.

in a red state, spell out the lesson here, map out the power
and water, or the rising lawn to disappear in

some fresh atlas, the new record.
practice wearing details yourself,
ghosted, twinned to a lighthouse.

movement in the dark requires geometry or optimism, a hand
along plaster, counting pockmarks.

streaked trees from the truck bed
the leaky world wets through
even this frame and mat

in the reeds, some insistent paper hum
in dragonflies mating, their drunken
swoop and hover.

the place where the land stopped and the water
began to green itself,

we walked here to talk about death,
to take off our pants.

you could ask me to push you in,
demand to be surprised,
your fierce mouth overflowing (bursting/bursting open).

the fine skin of a fever, bleaching. there's some paper, sit with it, a salt pig, a fuse, fresh slang, hitches in the running. tell amber in an evening; the plant, the factory we call to, trembles, a near-sweet burnt smell – name it, four or five ways at least.

~~maybe the only way to think is~~ what's cut is closer
to being still,
a pearly stream of fuel across the asphalt,
a peal – your hand a weapon,

just touching a plant or a child
in this place, just following orders, listening
well – that's where trouble waits.

welcome arrow, stippled like split bone,
the moon's nothing to pray over, a noun in the ear of the watchers

a dog bolts through in arc and amble,
clots of people weigh worry

wet nose against the back of a hand, a cool comma,
all moons are comparisons, possible constants, unflinching

this begins, quiet, craning.

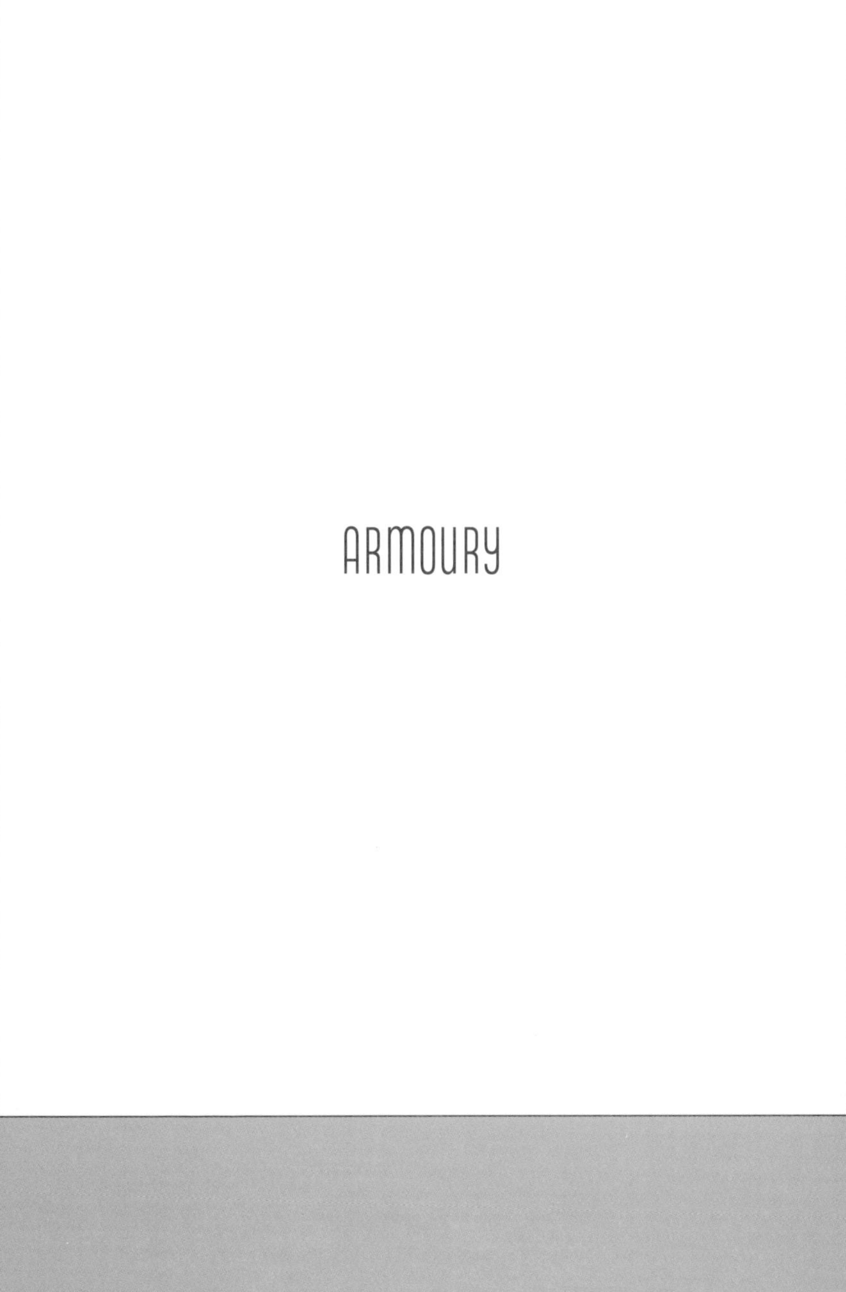

ARMOURY

Echo Chamber

You can tuck your whole hand neatly inside the pocket
of your cheek. Some girls can, anyway.
Here's one in a skinny kitchen in Ojai:
the slip of her fist as a minnow,
fine and quick past her incisors
to the wrist, shrugging,
no biggie, arm hooked to her face
like a tentacle or a hose.

There's a box labelled TEETH in this kitchen.
She touches the lid like it could do something special.
I haven't been here long – I don't even know
if teeth are inside, really, it's just a guess –
but I've never seen anything brave or
famous come from a tooth.

Even while the automated lawn starts
watering itself, ratcheting a stream
through the ink of the open window,
even as she stops up her infinity mouth,
even now, I won't open it.

Knife Fight, Glasgow

after David Gillanders

Your head wound was exquisite,
a sheet of red velvet
obscuring your eyes.

Here, the commonness
of household tools turning,
on circumstance, to active
meat in complex hallways,
the alcove of a payphone
where voices make demands
or even pray.

I touched the place your face
should have been, cradled
between the gloved hands
of the nurses'
quiet frame.

You Asked If It Was Something You Said

Last night in conversation, the full frame dislodged, a cloud held
your hair in loose knots as a promise. We woke to a thousand casualties
in Gaza, a place where they are running out of blood.

A computer screen in an empty office tower gave the news, the air
circulation filtering the sound of the cloud's breath. While I read
Al Jazeera, I wanted the crush of skin against my face, rich with sweat, alive.

At home, I eat simple food, make stiff drinks with my sister
and watch the sealed city sit like a smoking parcel in our kitchen.
No poems like ribbons today.

Snapshot

Marina, her
braceleted
wrist chops
and churns in
the rough barley,

a huge curling. Her
ghost-pale hair
threshed back, drops off
with drift, a slender
obligation of braid,
brush-whipped ellipsis,
gliding into the cut.

Armoury

A dress flatters when unzipped.
I'd ask for that much, to draw the tab down, lay bare
the swan of your spine, the glacial, slackening shoulder blades.

This hotel is powdered latex,
leather look-alike, neon, a nod
to sea or sugar. You took me here
for a two-minute melody anyone could manage,
even in psychedelic fripperies or a mask.

Your gown in party print
against the mirrored headboard.
Watch how it refracts.

Soft

after Winston Chmielinski

chart the ferrous,
prenatal repeats,

sputum, throat wound,
knuckle
into the tape deck,
kneel before the blip
in surprise –
sound his voice,
lean.

hours condensed
on the window,
pearling, tell
the beginning,
shaven knuckle into
wrist, cord-bound, dialing,
wall behind lit
like an out-of-focus grotto.

don't and toned
down in one room
at last, one folding the fire
blanket, the other akimbo.

still dangerous,
keeping reefed.

Draught

I haven't bothered to peel right down to the base paint, content that the impractical effort of layering velvet on gold-stamp has a flavour of rage to it. A matte sweepover, smoothed by palm effort, affected, nearly all pinks. This is reaching – all this fold and feather is listening and keeps swallowing. Things ring, things beep at the grim barricade of breakfast. I pass and it riffles amen, amen, ahem. It steps back, presses in.

One cough fits in the sealed envelope: thank him or the text written over. One container dreams another, nested quiet in the shipyard, and makes rote inquiries.

Which twist is best for the situation? I like sentences that begin singing, 'I, I, I,' loping up, hunched. I like my nervous mammal clauses, always shouldering the baseboards. Sometimes there can be more than one hard drop. I move my gleaning piece and everything rattles. The cobalt kitchen is flinty king of the afternoon and I am in it, scrubbing out the rosewater, carbon and cooked milk.

The Future

after Henry Darger

every thing is robust, these leaves,
white socks now falling forward in columns,

loops machinating over the field.
girls in knee-high clouds, ringlets,

girls like scattered improbable shrapnel,
dispersing towards the future in pairs and packs,
cutlasses drawn.

Calling Collect

hotel sleep
you and your devices
calibrating on the pillow,
apparently. circadian machines
loping through, little tick of corporeal hum, little current.

this used to be the region out of service – I have dreams, now,
aground, between every rock
a shoulder asking, some glass, furred nylon twine.

remember the tapes we made of each
other, thrown on the counter, the appeal
and pills, the deer of your voice
in the echo chamber, my van.

ink this part out:

payphone payphone payphone

canted in the gravel,
humming, drawing all the no-see-ums,
moths hurling themselves at the wolfish season,
lean, more teeth and curl,
the pencilled numbers on a wad of box top
in succession, dialed.

a transport passes, a world in the dark, blinking,
flat heat felt thickly on the face.

accosted, eaten, you punch
out numbers from within a sleeve.

collars were made for hands to ladder through.

a hesitation against industrial carpet
in the mezzanine
distends the breadth of the room.

think two thin bitten fingers, steam,
the draw of the soft count, one breath

then cut.

again: reverse,
from the top.

in the vulgar tongue,
ten days, some struggle,
hatching a few lines to wallpaper.

my bad skin, it breaks and falls off.
there is nothing to do but be dressed,
to pull on an outside, a shell
with no soundless inside, spouting blood.

creature possibility, blurred skulk
between cars or parts
of a road.

I got so excited at the coyote
by the cookie factory,
every day near the flag,
an unbrushed leaning,
until I realized it was a statue,
taxidermy or a territorial mark.
a body can be like that.

oh uncomfortable land,
dun slice whorled in dried whatever
that birds pick apart,
a cellphone ruined, spidered in
plastics, feathers of newsprint
falling open.

the close eye,
this animal's a mouthed name,
I'm a frayed-out anthem watching it,
a machine now,
watching back.

Hochelaga

The room spins out like a wet wig, a new kind of lure,
anorexic plaster sinking under itself.

Season of declarative statements,
one after another, coring all the apples,
thinking about the sound of ice across
a telephone line, or maybe just ice cubes,
nothing quite as grand as later glaciers.

Vanity records can't save anything,
but they still pinch the heart with popular disco hits in joual,
some face stuffed into the idea of a good idea.

Hang a sheet over the living room wall
to make a studio,
cut away the slab of afternoon and it's a little diorama
of some lesser saint
sandwiched in an arcane uniform,
an evening gown's blue volume
in afternoon light, catching
everything drop-jawed.

The Rye House

Rye House

Trouble –
it's mother and
just in view,
Mr. Stanley Wilson.

Sydney E. Young as Joe in *They Came to a City*, 1946

He had to kiss her, but it was staged;
you can hide a lot with your hands
when you stand close together.
His gabardine sleeves cancelled all the crepe,
made her disappear.

1:40 a.m at the Coronation Party

Come in from the lawn,
fix the bow in your hair and make
another show of the punch bowl
with orange and brandied cherries.
No one sees grass stains on satin.

Nov 1962

Syd Jr., Dad (Grandpa Young),
playing pool.
Dad's a real hustler,
pretends he don't know
how to play,
then fixes you.

Lake Ontario

New York State on the other side,
but you had turned away,
flicking a match into
the velvet frozen sand.

Son-in-Law Tony at Home, Sept 1973

Before he embarrasses himself
with the axe.

Third Date

She overlooked
his Northern Soul seven-inches stacked
on a nail in the rec-room panelling.

Uncle Bobby's Children's Hour, CFTO-TV

The universe here is slippers and tone.
Frank in a birdsuit made of boas
we got from a costume shop for dancing girls
slaps his ass off-camera,
trying to make me lose it.

Uncle Bill, Babysitter

Amateur entomologist
with a weekend interest in trepanning for better health.
He gave me a newsprint pocketbook about Jesus
flying a UFO, and we built a cardboard tray
to watch the solar eclipse without going blind.
We stood in the yard and held it together,
and it was the first time I remember being
afraid to look up.

New Year's Day

Her tender face seen through
the poinsettia that poisoned the cat.
Between us, the olive plate,
the pile of fatted bones
in scalloped porcelain,
our pattern.

END TIMES

A Formal Address

There's a gothic shape to the world,
a mess of feathers from the parking lot,
gathered and fanned to white.

To cook a ham, take the plastic wrap off first.
That's sound advice, but still,
anything that colour raises suspicion.
Anything that colour never looks done.

A man folds clothes at the laundromat:
ten black shirts, ten black slacks,
ten reverent knots of socks.

Her feet bled through the hose,
bobbled socks confettied
with maroon for days,
nails canted and cutting,
constant.

Moving beyond skin,
I wash everything.
Sterility becomes a handsome project,
iodine pools.

The clutch of December
is always Sudbury, getting carded,
the wedge of someone cotton-mouthing through
an approximation, the white edge,
a canine in the light.

Texas

coming down to rock and blot,
dawn, bone
inked thoroughly in bleak search,
the stripped name a sound, ditch,
slough, an alley,
maybe an island, half a cigarette tossed off.

creamed corn, one litre of cola,
sundae or something similar,
pound of ribs, dry-rubbed,
three nectarines, a peach,
sweet tea, saltines, untouched.

he walks, make statements after.

your clothing – no language
into the unit, memory
a sheet in the wind, tethered,
that snap, shoring,
shoring, just ashore.

the lights didn't dim. nothing.
swallow, arc, then just rifts.

who was watched, who was invited?

an indigo heel snapped off in the mud.
what colour left, I fill the blanks myself:

her no.

In Mimico

The prison clicks
into place, the crane lifts each little geometry,
nests it with like parts.

I want the dwelling
of a turn or a hammer,
a horse blurred in
the kitchen doorway, your laugh
summoning from the ditch.

This gets called the seam that holds pleats in.
Talk a wire through the dug-up din
then talk a grackle onto it
in profile, claw gripping briefly,
one lemon eye surveying.

New Testament

Splitting and projection – your basic drinking man's blues –
surface just comes off in your hand.
The labour of looking sets the hydro station ablaze.
Her brown wool dress, her belt and slip,
the teenage bible found in the woods,
all else, relentless.

The End Times

The photocopier is a good place to think
about avoiding the doctor.
Hunched here, crushing the spines of paperbacks
while thinly heaving, I don't want anyone
listening between my shirt and lungs,
except for maybe you.

The fluorescents hum.
My boss watches the news on the flat-screen by his desk,
talks about protesters like they're football hooligans or terrorists,
and I press the big green button on the machine,
consider my friend's hands
on webcam, trying to catch a moth in her room in England
while it darts beyond her reach then dive-bombs the screen.
An exclamation of pixilated wing too close for auto-focus,
auroral, then gone.

At the disco wake last night, I ordered a soda and grenadine,
but instead they gave me bitters, so I was drinking
raw salt and looking through swaths of grey balloons
waving like we were all underwater,
waiting for some bioluminescent fish
to swim between us and the fistfuls of glitter
and shredded paper. I didn't know him, really,
but I cried into my hand in the dark,
until I started coughing, standing there
in my yard-sale lingerie,
suddenly panicked at the thought of cellular division,
or forgetting your middle name.

Test Reel

Let their ribs stretch out – there is no figure
that is not also a ground in

its arctic plane. Cutting rooms, as luck
would have it, have academic sincerity.

Sincerities, the lit business of eyes,
having not used praise

for days, each snug category asleep, its own
Bermuda, a dream-walled theatre.

May 13

The abridged distance between these places
is cordoned in pedestrian time,
holding my shoes in the Buffalo airport
with no way to carry water.

Air Force One draws all peripheral,
any pane lined three deep with arcing arms,
camera phones pointed in open audience
this long morning.

On the tarmac, a man leaps,
his fists elastic against the air
in repetition, joy
that's embarrassing to stare at.

A Record

Terrible postcards from the anarchic hills,
the road hemmed twice with olive trees, desperate arms
flapping; you smile the fine sun through.

Your beads, a Cuban heel
to straighten,
'girl smokes' – the long ones,
one thigh, two, move like lanterns
or letters being walked out.

Video is cheap, perfect – the grain of a wall all
green glow, standing on the mattress in a rabbit mask with my placard,
the black mould like some broken edge to the tape, pocket-worn.
With colour values bled, every room
approximates a ward.

That bottle must have had a ship in it once,
now it's just a cast of water
at the bottom of an empty frame,
part of the mast still stuck to the sky.

Home Economics

Salmonella is a quiet encounter, I just want a bucket of bleach over the cutting board blush, streaked with slubs of fat, smelling like some lesser metal or a lab.

I have learned most practical lessons about dead animals from books; they give numbers and times. I can make gravy if I have to, debone, devein, render, keep things sharp. People marry for less than this.

Latex gloves before I pushed my hands inside the cavity of a death. There was the mess in mesh, an envelope of gizzard and giblets. I tried not to touch what I was touching, tried to think of my grandmother, the nonchalance of a heart in the sink, the cow's tongue, some small bird thawing to bossa nova.

I use needles for other tasks, normally. I can sew, so I used those skills to close the broken place. I covered it in fat and foil, rearranged the oven racks to fit a body trying to breach the burden of itself, overgrown.

Be Prepared

Make it pastoral, vermilion
script of barking and pulse.
Dead deer on the answering machine,
their skinned limbs a wealth of velvet
ribboned into piles.

It's diphenhydramine sometimes,
mostly just a habit of alcohol
leading to sleep.
The week is always a project,
slumped in the room, spreading.
I get nervous.

Yesterday, I dreamed
of standing in the wet leaves with a rifle,
trying to force the wrong calibre of bullets in.

OBSOLETE OBJECTS IN THE LITERARY IMAGINATION

Chapter Titles from *Obsolete Objects in the Literary Imagination*

i A Field Guide to Non-Absorbable Sutures

ii Ditches in Greenstone

iii Cutlines: Their Purpose and Maintenance

iv Representations of the Bluenose in Late-Twentieth-Century Canadian Postage

v Basic Sundress Alteration

vi Her [redacted]

What This Is About

Every slot in this building
holds a body at a computer
asking questions about expiry dates;
every mix has a lean
stretch.

Rejected stoneware
on a box beside the dumpster
set up like an offering – on this street
someone is always saying, *Enough*.
No more Florida, no more
obligations of wicker or lacquer
in the chapter on minimalism.

First, Confused Examples

In the yard with the plastic drum
after picking berries,
a recipe gleaned, half-
blotted on the card,
gestures at citrus,

the stolen rum –
she laughed, something
like fire in what you
did when you opened
your eyes.

Making Decisions To Proceed

after Alice Oswald

Time-lapsed smoke coiled back
towards your pursed *oh*
channels silence.

I am bound to the balcony; a door
in the sidewalk heaves open, pigeons lifting,
the day on its ear already

over the good bread, plateful of seeds
to slick my thumb through.
Please, give me any ending but drift,
away on my bicycle, singing
obscenity dry.

So much happens in small boxes,
the hole in the roof must travel far for the light
and my eyes are common stones,
my mouth a torn circular, my hair
severed, left to the grass,
blown up in little hash marks.

Now there is nothing but counting,
logic moving heavy
alongside my body as it leaves
itself, leaves the street,
runs red.

Genealogy

Reel and candle bulb,
short them both.

Forget, think first on fire wounding the wall,
sending this up in a thick sheet, so quiet in the road
scraping our thighs,
evidence of all sinners here: vowels,
formaldehyde, pancake in a limited range of shade melting,
melting in its pans, simply contained, simmering
little complaints, far from lifelike, we can surely agree
on this building, lit, graduating to an apparition of ash, lilies
gathered, culled, refused.

Trees retreat, gasping; we lean in,
the afternoon unlaces.

Not To Be Too Sharply Distinguished

The pendant lamp measured out the table,
just glasses snuck in and suggested full sentences
left sloppy against each other,
her red shoes tipped in at the door.

She walked her eyeliner all the way down to the elevator,
counting categories after silence.
I nodded, went along with it,
kept my hands to themselves.

Some Twenty-First-Century Novel

Reason might as well be a shirt sleeve
scissored free for the bar photograph.

Summer, your raw shear
is insistent,
though only in double kick drum,
phone cards, birth control,
clippers loosed on the floor
when his fingers fed
my pause,
humming animals,
mimicking.

Praising and Disparaging the Functional

This is how a string of ghosts appears in your inbox,
and this is how you answer each of them,

          always, little sails.

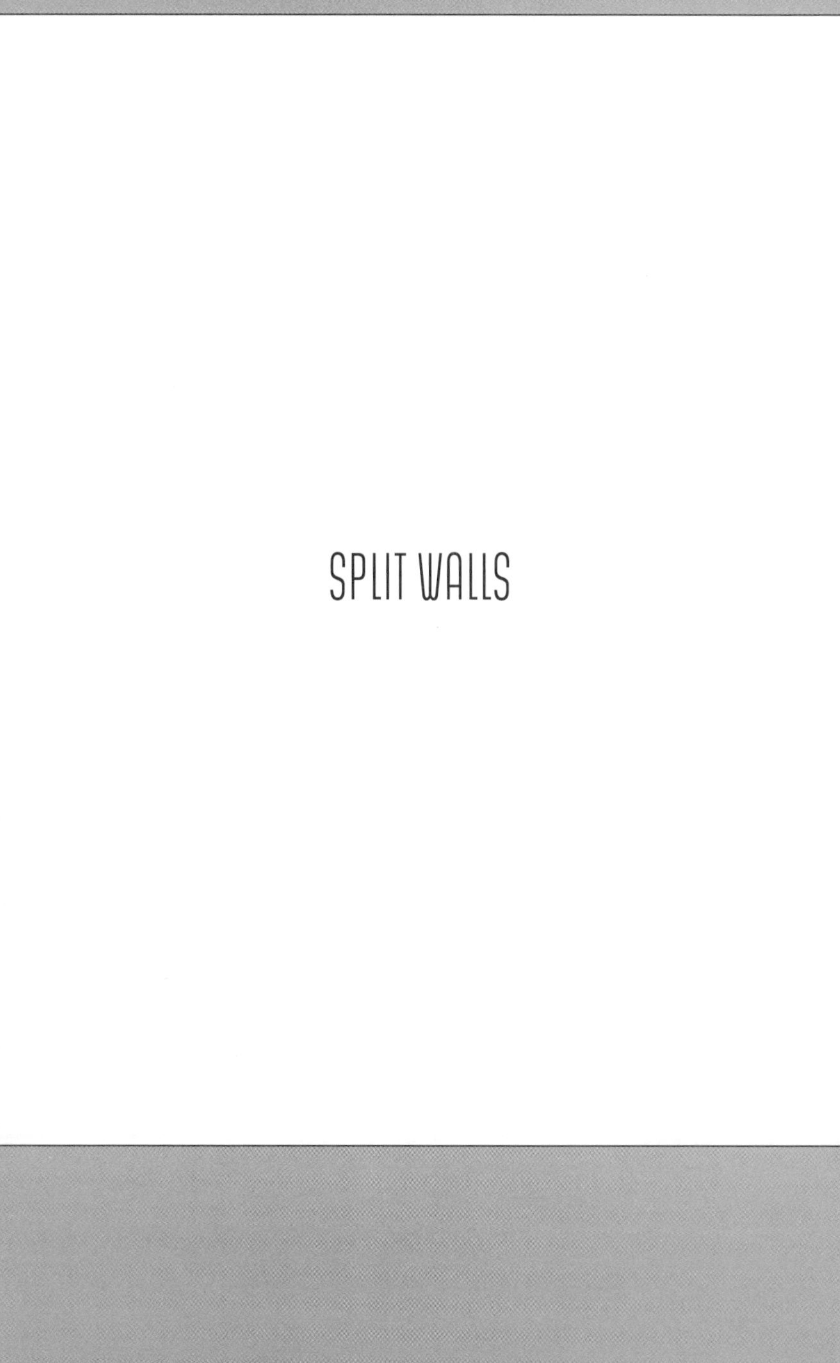

SPLIT WALLS

Send Money

Across the street, wig mountain,
soft mountain, the name for your mother,
an anonymous plume I hope to understand in a few months.

I've sent you several cities – pick the one you like best.
They all come with hot pink script, knife sharpening,
subdivided labour, and all the laundry
and froth caused by moving, mandated parts.

This is just a note from another close green order and its hysteria.
I folded a receipt into quarters,
chewed a hole in its centre, then held it in front of my glasses
and the nets,
I thought about your calluses long enough to fan my hand
and snap a photo of all the countable tendons.

There are one hundred twenty-one actions required
for disassembly, the generous smell of flaring,
always wet, sweet steps
towards tertiary bins in plastic and stainless.
You want me to tell you about them?
I really want to. Send stamps, send money,
we'll talk.

Visitation

Our lovely vices, we had them in boxes, in practice, gamy and warm in foam. In the room with fire and the offering, we had plastic cups and juice in fat plastic bottles that dimpled when pouring. There was so much work; we sawed and burnt.

There were spongy buns with parsley attached to my hands like prostheses, and crustless sandwiches with creamed meats. There were circles to walk in, names to crawl under.

You backstitched and made a waxy announcement, same-same. The sound dilated. Your teeth clacked. The books closed as soft doors, turned fine.

It was a pageant of modelled architectures, trays of them, and paper to cut, a proofed stun backwards into the practical.

The Tender Places Are Still the Ones with Knives

Two people
on the sidewalk, pants undone,
each in the solitary slouch
of tucking shirttails, elbow-close,
returned, turning away.

Current

because we turned to the sound of water
in the stairwell,
and put our minds to the idea of a river,
we found what was running underground.

on a street of copper, wanting, and felled by lightning,
split sequins littered the shingles that shored up
a chorus of promises,
magpies and crows in solvent pitch.

TWO SUITES AFTER
FRANCIS BACON

after *Triptych Inspired by the Oresteia of Aeschylus* (1981)

i

tell the poured concrete,
tell the wood room, the roach,
the pine beetle clipping the air,
swerving in the thin light
that gets through this
half-nested shell

ii

we stored horror,
cupboard made of plywood
ghosted with jars accruing grey,
the pile of rusted lids hung on string,
swung

iii

little pills
of Styrofoam crumbling from the corners
behind the chained stove,
little piles of movie snow,
her weather, her air

after *Triptych* (1987)

i

uninterrogated elbow
leaning on an afternoon

ask back after it,
yard unhemmed,
seeding out, flaming

ii

hinged, a crook,
the soft cave
pollen powdered,
yellow as pesticide

iii

a litter of envelopes aside

animal practice, bloom
of rind, chalk to mark an outline

the split wall, the different
ways a body whistles, breathes

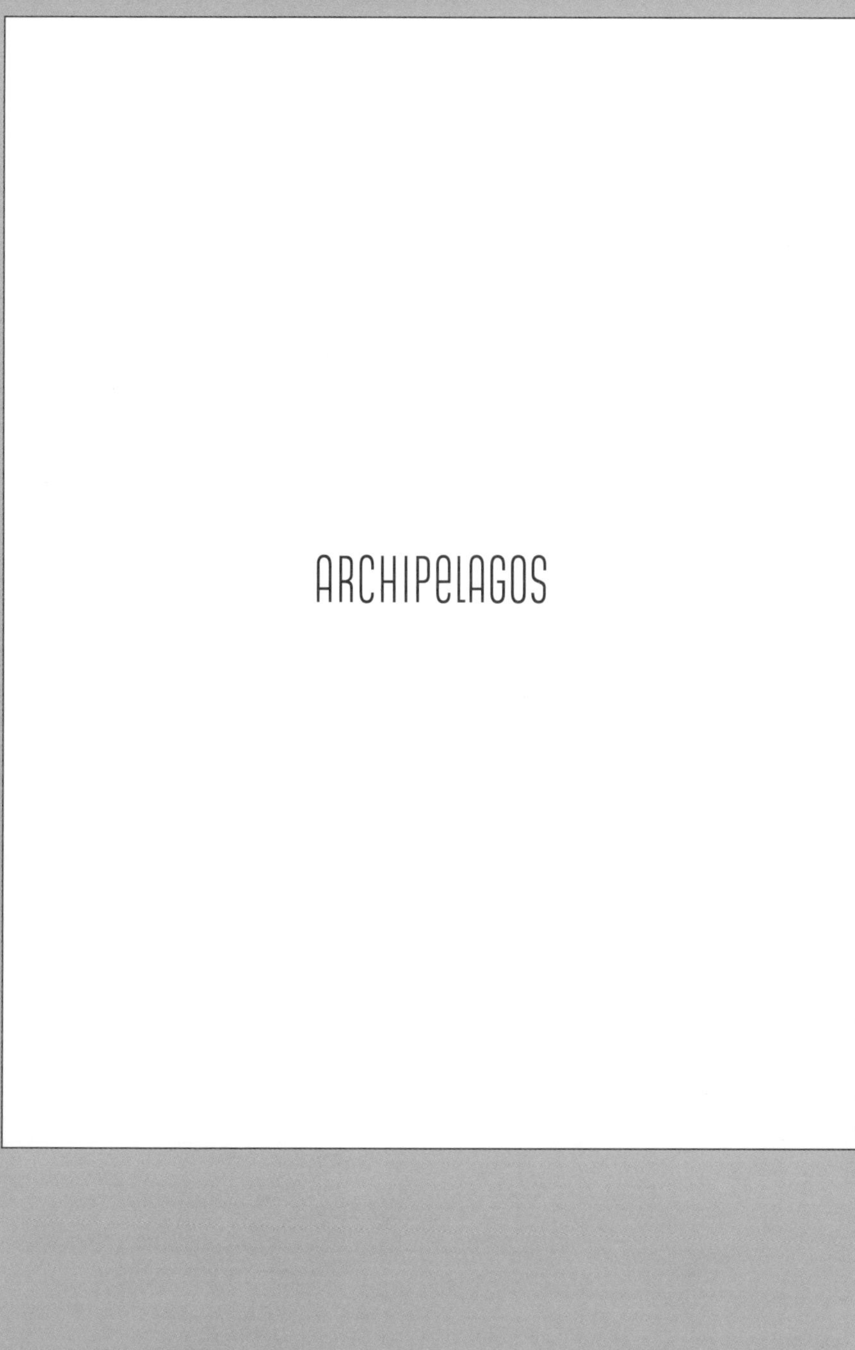

ARCHIPELAGOS

before a wealth of windows
waiting to take off belt and watch
with the hope of few official questions,
scan bone-through, transparent
before you're cradled in the air

over the twice-tossed glass
landscape, tearing a little
packet of salt, spilling it over
the tray table,
dusting your knees.

dear bird,

here in arms

is there enough
to just explode already?
the blue, clean line of land
precise, only crooked.

each night I dream the neighbourhood
as an obstacle course stopping me
from catching a train.

it is never this city,
and often my little legs seem almost mechanical.

I can be hours away from the station
with the final call flashing and I still try.

never really miss, never catch it,

just bolt up, clattering
awake.

when I was a girl, I had a postcard
from a married man,

a photograph of a mirror
that turned the room into a bowl,
brittle curtains raked into weedy filter.

the following effects:

one dubbed blues tape
on the mantle,
the joke of a logoed ball cap,

his thumb, an eclipse
in frame,
opening the eye
that recorded
while dodging his reflection out,

giving, grim –

he'd fled.

I will promise this short-shrift season
in video and voicemail from Toronto,
to ride past the chop shop, detailing
the concrete with wet wheels.

making a meal of single servings,

you lie in long grass and break melba toasts in honey against your palate,

a twist of rebar prodding your shoulder blade.

the scorched-out

scatters itself in dust, airbrushed through
        thistles puffed into seed,

little worn-through heel of fire,

not melting, but streaking the glass shards it's ringed with.

enough of the passport-sized photos,
backless, scanned on screen,
no dregs of ink smeared flathand
across the waxy paper,

enough of just scrolling,
never ceasing to scroll.

what was looking when there wasn't
a date stamp that kept rolling in live feed?

even refresh was a tread in thickness, then,

clicking through to another slow-loading version of another girl's bedroom when it required anticipatory pause:

a sliced couch or quarter-window

blur of an eye, hairfall,
enough bra strap to give you the glimpse
of an other on the line.

I guess this is supposed to be exciting.

we are entering a story in the middle. it creeps up your pant legs
on your way to the video mart
where you will read boxes,
try to pick a tone that won't leave you
envious or haloed.

in straight-to-video of the neighbourhood you once lived in,
crying and grey are motifs.
every fifteen minutes there is a slow pan to rooftops –

you laugh, then are covered in crumbs,
fleas bouncing off your ankles, shaking it all off.

the back acre holds all his cars and heavy machinery; take your wrench
and strip what you want before the snow seals all the doors shut.

the buttoned-in blue light, the magnetized reel clicking
into record.

brushes against
the entrance,
flares.

they pulp tissue that isn't called meat, cook it down, but this is before the hot water process, when it is still a metal thought and pink, fluffy sludge. what gets you the most is the idea of chipping up hooves, the sound of cuticle shredding.

that photo makes you stop: marshmallow heart.

she wiped each foot against her shins before she got under the blankets. stopped. wiped them again. mid-morning, still thick with her sleep, I swept around the bed, swimming the broom over divots, like a quiet third breath in the room.

I gasp sometimes, in public,
waist-deep in
strained embroidery snarl,
indent of teeth along a thigh –

queuing in a public line
at shell-white hours,
there's the watery knot of an ankle in a sheet,

stirring itself down, snapping me right shut.

I can't buy stamps like that.

I can't predict her sewing a little sash of curses as she burns herself with the hot iron – how that sound careens out into the blank field I inherited while standing somewhere, seized.

deciduous teeth, little warm-water canines.

mornings disintegrate
a bolt, laceration
and stringing up,
pinned at the ankle.

chemical wash
you're suited for,

heels in snow, relief as something you wade through
that makes the performance of arching
more daring or arcane.

little exclamations,
little darts with drag, depending.

aerosol in your bachelor, big cans, enough to make the parquet tacky. a soft unsealing with every step to slap the radiator and let out pressure, wrench it open 'til it leaks and hisses furiously, blooming the window to clear.

like the common mouse.
like a quarter-fold.
like the elliptical turn of saying *Rattus rattus*.
like the steel storm door found in the ditch and brought home, mounted;
the thin tear in the screen, a flapping mouth.
like seafoam, julep.
the click of the card catalogue drawer.
like your love of a good index.

stay on the ball, girl,
keep yourself unskimmed.

walk the neon field,
royalled sulphur sublime,
the flattened land ribboned to win.

pick there,
coat your fingers, watch a lone partridge wobble-neck
through the Labrador tea, the mint and blackberry cane.

why not be the dust
spiralling up behind any claim –

unbraid your hair in a rut in the road, work it out thin in your hands,
walk back slowly to your name spoken aloud.

hands, claws,
Bakelite bangles clicking
together like teeth.

take me to the yaw of window,
the water-borne house in the drifting winter lot
cascading out of itself.

wrist cocked,
one reel of clothes in hand
unlocked frame by frame

unpredictable floral, poorly laid, slubbed his periphery.

it made me want to sound out vowels carefully, practice untying
my apron single-handed like a waltz step,
take up singing, be a lamb in a picture of Jesus, not
like rooms occupied with hatchet and rope,
the gutting knife and sweating, plated grey.

I wanted to keep feeding the mouth in front of me.
I wanted to be sweet.

one quiet year and a girl gets nervous,

as in breathless, as in running,

as in tickets to warm places
where weeds always thrive: archipelagos.

in a small bed, I rewrite my lines,
lean my hand to your jaw in reverse, listen:

the floor in drop cloths
suddenly remarkable, shrouded.

you dream you see a string tied to the roof
and walk into the leaves in the yard,
pulling until it comes free like foamcore, loosed
from the frame and floating up –

the roughed-out moon in watercolour
dusk, tethered low, still rising.

Notes and Acknowledgements

'Fuel' is for Chy Ryan Spain, who lies awake at night thinking about the same things I do.

'Texas' uses material from the Texas Department of Criminal Justice's Victim Services Brochure, Information Regarding Scheduled Executions (2005), and the words 'creamed corn … pound / of ribs, dry-rubbed' are from Michael Pfaendtner's documentary *Texas Hospitality* (2003).

'The End Times' was written after Will Munro's passing, in May 2010. Though I didn't know him personally, his community-building in Toronto reminds me that the city we dream of is also the city we can make for ourselves.

The following texts from David Beech's anthology *Beauty* (Whitechapel Press, 2009) were read, referenced and dissected through the creation of 'Test Reel':

Araeen, Rasheen. 'Cultural Imperialism: Observations on Cultural Situation in the Third World' (1976) 175–179.

Bernstein, Jay. 'Beauty and the labour of mourning' (1992). 101–106.

Derrida, Jacques. 'The sans of the pure cut' (1978). 82–88.

Golub, Leon and Nancy Spero. 'Interview with Adrian Searle' (1990). 189-192.

Hutchinson, Mark. 'Nausea: Encounters with Ugliness' (2002). 152–155.

Jones, Caroline A. 'The discourse of the studio meets the technological sublime' (1996). 131–136.

Richter, Gerhard. 'Notes' (1985). 180–182.

'Be Prepared' is for Matt Lennox.

The titles in 'Obsolete Objects in the Literary Imagination' are chapter titles (or modified chapter titles) from the book of the same name by Francesco Orlando (Yale University Press, 2006). 'Praising and Disparaging the Functional' is for Lauren Corman.

'archipelagos' is for Jason Burton, and includes my slant rehashing of a dream Wil Murray posted as a Facebook status update.

Early versions of 'In Mimico' and 'soft' appeared in *J Journal* and *Poetry Is Dead* respectively. 'The Future' appeared in the Henry Darger–themed zine *Mad as a Bad Tornado*, edited by Jean McEwan.

Thanks to the Ontario Arts Council for a grant that gave me time to work on this manuscript.

These poems have benefitted from the eyes of Roo Borson, Margaret Christakos and Kevin Connolly. I thank them for their attentive editing and patient mentorship. Also, I appreciate the close readings that friends and colleagues gave early drafts of these poems, for answering many of my questions and giving me new ones to chew on.

Thanks to the folks who've been supporting my zines over the past decade.

Gratitude goes to my family and friends for taking such good care of me, especially while I took care of this. I love you very much. Thanks in particular to Daniel Marrone, my favourite co-conspirator, for his inexhaustible enthusiasm, and to my parents, Robert and Pamela Pinder.

This book is dedicated to Miriam Pinder, always full of grace.

Sarah Pinder grew up along the north shore of Lake Superior. She now calls Toronto home.

Typeset in Aragon and Gala

Printed in August 2012 at the old Coach House on bpNichol Lane in Toronto, Ontario, on Zephyr Antique Laid paper, which was manufactured, acid-free, in Saint-Jérôme, Quebec, from second-growth forests. This book was printed with vegetable-based ink on a 1965 Heidelberg KORD offset litho press. Its pages were folded on a Baumfolder, gathered by hand, bound on a Sulby Auto-Minabinda and trimmed on a Polar single-knife cutter.

Edited by Kevin Connolly
Designed by Alana Wilcox and Leigh Nash
Author photo by Cristine Renna

Coach House Books
80 bpNichol Lane
Toronto ON M5S 3J4
Canada

416 979 2217
800 367 6360

mail@chbooks.com
www.chbooks.com